I0011212

About the Au

Mrs. Susan Thomas has 8 years of experience in QTP. She has developed automation frameworks using QTP for large software testing projects. She is strong in VBScript and VBA.

She has worked on projects in below domains.

1. Investment Banking
2. Healthcare
3. Logistics
4. Mortgage Banking
5. Retail Banking

Her hobbies are travelling to new tourist places, watching football, cricket and learning latest technological stuff.

Preface

QTP (now UFT) is the industry leading tool in automation testing space. Just knowing record and playback in QTP is not enough in large testing projects having 1000+ test cases.

We must know best practises used in automation testing frameworks. This book is for QTP engineers who want to design the automation frameworks in QTP. This book contains complete source codes and examples in QTP.

Major topics covered in this book are.

1. Automation Testing Frameworks in QTP.
2. Data driven automation frameworks(DDF).
3. Keyword driven automation frameworks(KDF).
4. Hybrid driven automation frameworks(HDF).
5. Generating graphical reports in QTP.
6. Using Excel Sheet to store test data.
7. Handling Exceptions for uninterrupted execution.
8. Writing Generic functions to increase reusability.

1. Test Automation frameworks 4

   1.1 Test Automation - Introduction 4
   1.2 Test Automation Frameworks - Introduction 4
   1.3 Why Test Automation framework? 5
   1.4 Types of Automation framework 6
   1.5 Which framework to choose? 6

2. Data driven Automation framework 8

   2.1 Data Driven Automation Framework 8
   2.2 When to use Data driven automation framework 9

3. Keyword driven Automation framework 11

   3.1 Test Data 17
   3.2 Keyword Library (Function Library) 20
   3.3 Main driver script 27
   3.4 Object Repository 38
   3.5 Reporting 41

4. Hybrid Automation framework 48

   4.1 Hybrid framework Introduction 48
   4.2 Hybrid framework features 48

5. Utility Functions in frameworks 49

   5.1 Reading Excel File in QTP. 49
   5.2 Changing the date format 50
   5.3 Writing Data to Text File 52
   5.4 Associating Library file to QTP Test 53
   5.5 Associating Object Repository file to QTP Test 55
   5.6 Closing processes by Name 56
   5.7 Sending an email from framework 57
   5.8 Taking a screenshot in QTP. 58
   5.9 Importing excel sheet to datatable in qtp 59
   5.10 Exporting the datatable sheets 60
   5.11 Loading ini file in QTP 61

1. Test Automation frameworks

In this chapter, you will learn about the test automation and why we should use the framework and what are the types of automation frameworks out there to choose from.

1.1 Test Automation - Introduction

Test automation is the process of automating the manual testing activities. When the software is ready for test, we can verify and validate it either manually or by automation. If the software is huge with lot of modules in it, We need many testers to test it. Whenever there is a change in the software, We will have to again test it to verify that it meets the requirements and there is no defect in it.

Manually Testing the application has below disadvantages.
1. Time consuming
2. Costly
3. Cumbersome
4. Quality not assured due to human mistakes
5. Time constraints
6. Repeatative and hence Boring

By automating the testing process, we can overcome above challenges in testing process. You can use any tool like QTP , QTP or Test Complete etc. In this book, we are going to use QTP tool.

1.2 Test Automation Frameworks - Introduction

Well – now that you know why automation is required in software testing, it is a time to understand the best practises used in test automation industry. As of 2014, QTP is the most popular automation testing tool in the market followed by TestComplete and QTP. The striking difference between QTP and QTP is that QTP is open source tool which only supports Web application testing.

While QTP is a licensed tool offered by HP and it supports wide variety of desktop applications built in .Net, Java along with Web applications.

QTP is used to automate applications developed in wide variety of environments like .Net, Java, PeopleSoft, Siebel, Web application. That's what makes QTP the most varsatile tool in the market today.

 Now let us define the term – **Automation Framework**. The automation framework is nothing but the set of guidelines and conventions to follow when designing the code to test the software. When we follow these guidelines while developing the automation code, it helps to make automation testing more beneficial and scalable.

A test automation framework is an integrated system that sets the rules of automation of a specific product. This system integrates the function libraries, test data sources, object details and various reusable modules. These components act as small building blocks which needs to be assembled to represent a business process. The framework provides the basis of test automation and simplifies the automation effort.

1.3 Why Test Automation framework?

Since many tools provide record and playback feature, People usually rely on it. But this is not a good practise. When the project is very big consisting of lot of modules, it is very important to have a automation framework in place.
The automation framework provides below advantages.

1. Proper oraganisation of test data.
2. Automation of new test cases is fast and simple.
3. Custom HTML or Excel reports along with Charts.
4. High Code Reusability.
5. Easy to maintain and enhance.
6. Easy to learn.

1.4 Types of Automation framework

There are many kinds of automation frameworks based upon the testing phase like Unit testing and System testing. Here is the list of **Unit testing frameworks**.

1. Junit (Java)
2. TestNG (Java)
3. Nunit (C#.Net)
4. unittest (Python)
5. Test::Unit (Ruby)

Here is the list of **System testing frameworks.**

1. Data Driven Framework
2. Keyword Driven Framework
3. Hybrid Framework (Data + Keyword)

Unit testing frameworks are used by developers to test the software. As a system tester, our job is to test the system as a black box. So here on we will be discussing only about system testing automation frameworks.

1.5 Which framework to choose?

We have to consider below factors when selecting the framework.

1. Size of the application
2. Time Constraints
3. Budget Constraints

2. Data driven Automation framework

In this chapter, you will learn about how to design data driven automation frameworks in QTP.

2.1 Data Driven Automation Framework

In data driven frameworks, we store the test data seperately in the excel sheet and then we repeat the testing of each test data candidate with same code.

Below example will demonstrate how we can use data driven framework in QTP.

Suppose we have a web application where in User will have to choose the User Id while doing the registration. The user Id should comply with below rules.

1. It should be at least 8 characters in length.
2. It should contain at least one Upper case alphabet character.
3. It should contain at least one digit.
4. It should not contain # character.

To test this feature, we can create the test data as shown in below figure and then write the code in QTP to pick up one User Id at a time and try to do the registration.

	A	B	C	D	E
1	TestID	UserID	Expected Result	Actual Result	Test Status
2	1	test1	Reject		
3	2	test17889	Reject		
4	3	tesT9080	Accept		
5	4	tesT#080	Reject		

Figure 1 - Sample Test Data Sheet

As shown in previous figure, we have created the test data sheet containing different User IDs we want to test. We have also mentioned which User Ids should be accepeted by the System and which ones should be rejected.

The excel sheet after the execution is shown below.

	A	B	C	D	E
1	TestID	UserID	Expected Result	Actual Result	Test Status
2	1	test1	Reject	Rejected	Pass
3	2	test17889	Reject	Rejected	Pass
4	3	tesT9080	Accept	Accepted	Pass
5	4	tesT#080	Reject	Accepted	Fail

Figure 2 - Sample Test Data after execution

From QTP script, we can read each row in the excel sheet and test the user Id one by one. Based upon the actual result, we can mark the test status as Pass or Fail as shown in previous figure. We are going to see how to read excel sheet data from QTP in next chapters.

2.2 When to use Data driven automation framework

We can use data driven frameworks when

1. The features to test are very less.
2. We have to automate the test cases very fast.

3. Application size is very small.
4. We have to test the same functionality with lot of combinations of the test data.

3. Keyword driven Automation framework

In this chapter, you will learn about how to design keyword driven automation frameworks in QTP.

The keyword driven automation framework that we are going to develop will have below folder structure.

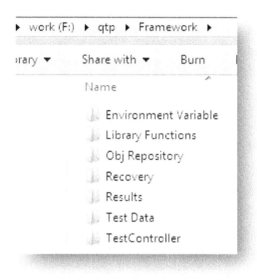

Figure 3 - Folder Structure of Framework

Details of the folders are given below.

1. **Environment Variables**

   This folder Contains ini file. We can store all environment variables in this file. For example – we can store the user id and password of the application under test in this file.

We also use ini file to specify the test data sheet path where our automated test cases are stored.

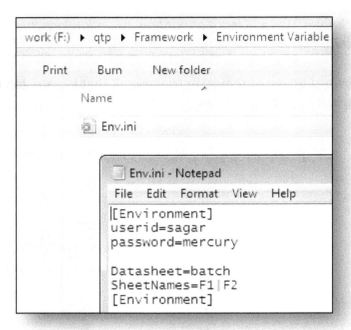

2. **Library Functions**

   This folder contains library (vbs/txt/qfl) files. In this framework, I have created 4 vbs files which contain the functions to perform specific operation. We can have any number of vbs files in the framework based upon the size of the application. We may group the functions in single vbs file based upon modules.

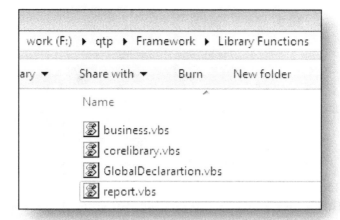

Business.vbs will store the functions that perform specific operation in the application. For example – we can have a login function which will take the input from the datasheet and try to login. Similarly we can have a function to book a trade/ticket.

Corelibrary.vbs will store the driver script and other generic functions to enter the data and verify the data in the application.

GlobalDeclaration.vbs will store all global variables that we will be using in the framework. For example – pass/fail counters of the test cases.

Report.vbs will store the functions that help us in creating the html reports and create charts based upon the execution status.

3. **Obj Repository**
   This folder will store the shared object repository of the application under test.

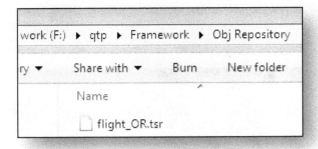

4. **Recovery**

   This folder contains the .qrs files for storing recovery scenarios. As of now, I have not added in recovery scenario in this folder.

5. **Results**

   This folder is going to store all html reports we are going to create.

   As shown in below figure, we have date folders in the results folder. So we store the reports by date. We have also used css file for styling the html report.

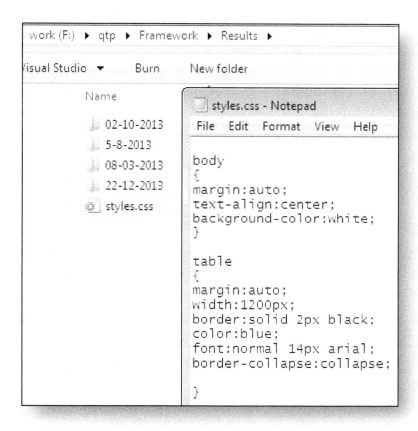

6. Test Data

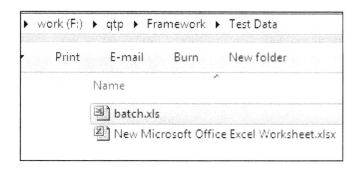

Test data folder stores the automated test cases in the excel sheet. We are going to have a look at this data sheet in later chapters.

7. **TestController.**
   This is the QTP test. It contains action1 containg call to the main driver script.

In general, the Keyword driven framework has 5 main components as shown below.

1. Keyword Library
2. Test Data Sheet(Test Cases)
3. Driver Script
4. Object Repository
5. Reporting (HTML Reports)

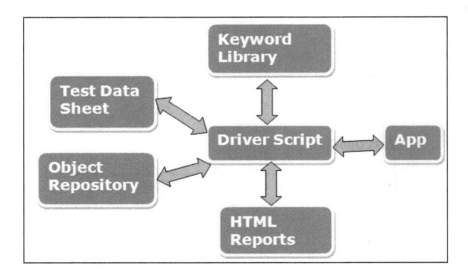

Figure 4 - Keyword Driven Framework Components

Let's have a look at each of these components.

3.1 Test Data

We validate the requirements of the software by executing test cases. Each test case has specific number of steps. We can convert these manual steps into automation by writing the functions to perform specific operations.

Sample Test data sheet is shown in below figure. The important columns in this excel sheet are mentioned below.

1. ID – Unique test case Id
2. Test Case Name – Test Case Name
3. Execution Flag – to Execute or not to execute test case
4. Test Step Id – Step id of the test case
5. Test Case Steps – Step name
6. Business Keyword – Business Keyword (Mapped to method)
7. ObjectTypes – Class Types of the controls like webedit, weblist, webbutton
8. ObjectNames – Names of the controls linktext:Next;linktext:Previous;linktext:Back
9. ObjectValues – Values to enter /operation to perform on control
10. Parameter1 – parameter to control the method flow
11. Parameter2 – parameter to control the method flow
12. Parameter3 – parameter to control the method flow

	A	B	C	D	E	F
1	ID	test_case_name	Exec_Flag	Test_step_ID	Test_case_steps	keyword
2	1	insert order	Y	step1	login	login
3				step2	insertorder	insertorder
4	2	fax order	N	step1	login	login
5				step2	insertorder	insertorder
6				step3	faxorder	faxorder
7	3	Delete order	N	step1	login	login
8				step2	insertorder	insertorder
9				step3	faxorder	deleteorder

Figure 4 – Test Data Sheet (Columns A-F)

G	H	I	J	K
objectTypes	objectnames	objectvalues	parameter1	parameter2
winedit;winedit;w	Agent Name:;f	sagar;mercury;click		
winedit;winedit	id;pwd	sagar;mercury		
winedit;winedit	id;pwd	sagar;mercury		

Figure 5 - Test Data Sheet (Columns G-K)

Each manual test case is converted to automation test case as shown in above figure. Each automated step corresponds to the method.

If any of the test step of the test case fails, whole test case will fail. So to mark the test case as pass, you should have all the steps of the test cases passed. Main driver script will read each row in the data sheet one by one and call the corresponding method (keyword) which will perform specific operation on the given elements on the webpage.

18

Column name Business Keyword is mapped to the function in the function (Keyword) Library in QTP script. So you will have to write the function for each keyword.
This is very important part of the framework. There are 2 steps involved in this process.

1. Identify the Keywords in Application
2. Write the code to perform that operation in QTP.

Example – Let us consider a bus ticket booking application where users can login, search buses, select tickets, book tickets, make the payment, view booking history, view profile etc.

Now identifying the keywords is very easy. Each operation that perform in the application could be a good candidate for the keyword. In our example, we can have below keywords.

1. Login
2. Search_Buses
3. Select_Tickets
4. Book_Tickets
5. Make_Payment
6. View_Booking_History
7. View_Profile

When we identify the keywords, we also need to identify the parameters that these keywords take.

For example – For login keyword, We will need 2 parameters that is user id and password.
For Search_Buses keyword, we will need 3 parameters that is source city, destination city and Travel date.

We can pass these parameters from the data sheet. The function mapped to this keyword will use these parameters and enter values in the application. If the data entry is successful, it will return true else it will return false.

In next section, we will see more about how to write functions.

3.2 Keyword Library (Function Library)

Keyword library contains 2 kinds of functions.
1. Application specific functions.
2. Framework related generic functions.

Sample Application specific functions are given below.
1. Login
2. BookTrade

Below is the source code of sample login function in **business.vbs** file. The function returns true or false. If it returns true, that means the keyword steps passes else it fails and subsequently the test case also fails.

```
'*********************************************
'Function Name  :- login
'Function Description :- login
'Develeoped by :- qtp-interview-
questions.blogspot.com
'*********************************************


Function login()

'launch application

      SystemUtil.Run "C:\Program
Files\Mercury Interactive\QuickTest
Professional\samples\flight\app\flight4
```

```
a.exe","","C:\Program Files\Mercury
Interactive\QuickTest
Professional\samples\flight\app\","open
"
      Set gActiveObject =
Dialog("Login")

'enter the data in login window using
setGenericFieldValues.

      setGenericFieldValues()


      If Window("Flight
Reservation").exist(11) Then
                login = true
                  Call
CreateTestCaseLog("Login   was
successful", 1)
      Else
                login = false
                Call
CreateTestCaseLog("Login   was not
successful", 2)
      End If


End Function
```

Sample Framework Related functions are given below.
1. EnterDate
2. VerifyData

3. GetTimeDiff

In out framework, We have stored the global variables in **GlobalDeclarartion.vbs** file as shown below.

```
Dim GstrObjectType, GstrObjectName,
GstrObjectValues,GstrParameter1,
GfileStamp,GtestCaseLog
Dim dtRows, intTotalRows,
intTestCaseCount, intFailCount,
tmpDataTbl
```

In our framework, we have stored generic functions in **corelibrary.vbs** file. The generic functions are called inside business functions. This increases the reusability. For example – login function uses setGenericfieldvalues function to enter the values in user id and password editboxes.

For example – below function will be used to enter data in any object like editbox, dropdown in the application. Please go through each line of the code as it is very important function. This function works on 3 global variables.

1. Object Types
2. Object Names
3. Object Values

We can pass as many object details as we want from the excel sheet seperated by the semi-colon(;).

For Example – if we pass below information from the excel sheet, setGenericfieldvalues function will enter the data in 2 editboxes with names in the object repository as Agent Name: and Password:. In editbox having name Agent Name:, value

Thomas will be entered. :. In editbox having name Password:, value mercury will be entered and finally it will click on the button with name Ok.

objectTypes	objectnames	objectvalues
winedit;winedit;winbutton	Agent Name:;Password:;ok	thomas;mercury;click

```
'* * * * * * * * * * * * * * * * * * * * * * * * * * * * * * * * * * * * * * * *
'Function Name :- setGenericfieldvalues
'Function Description :- sets the data
in UI
'Develeoped by :- qtp-interview-
questions.blogspot.com
'* * * * * * * * * * * * * * * * * * * * * * * * * * * * * * * * * * * * * * * *

Public function setGenericFieldValues()

'Flag to store pass / fail status
    blnoverallreturnvalue=true

'Split the object Names with ; in case
there are multiple objects
    If instr(gObjectNames,";")>0 Then

'Split object types variable with ;

arrObjectTypes=split(gObjectTypes,";")

'Split object Names variable with ;
arrObjectNames=split(gObjectNames,";")
```

```
'Split object values variable with ;

arrObjectValues=split(gObjectValues,";"
)

        Else

'In case there is a single object,
convert the variable into arrays.

arrObjectNames=array(gObjectNames)

arrObjectTypes=array(gObjectTypes)

arrObjectValues=array(gObjectValues)

   End If

 'The ubound of 3 arrays should be same
    If
(ubound(arrObjectTypes)=ubound(arrObjec
tNames) and
ubound(arrObjectTypes)=ubound(arrObject
Values)) Then

'For loop to work with each object one
by one
        For i=0 to
ubound(arrObjectTypes)
                blnreturnvalue=true
```

```
activecontrol=trim(arrObjectNames(i))

curvalue=trim(arrObjectValues(i))


'Switch to the code based upon object
type.
            Select Case
ucase(trim(arrObjectTypes(i)))

          Case "WINEDIT"


gActiveObject.WinEdit(activecontrol).se
t curvalue

          Case "WINBUTTON"


gActiveObject.WinButton(activecontrol).
click



          Case "WINCOMBOBOX"

              If
gActiveObject.WinButton(activecontrol).
exist Then
```

```
gActiveObject.WinButton(activecontrol).
select curValue
                    Call
createTestCaseLog("Value selected from
combo box",1)

blnreturnvalue=true

                        Else


blnReturnvalue=false

                    Call
createTestCaseLog(activecontrol &"-
combobox does not exist",2)
                End If


        End Select

        If blnreturnvalue=false
Then


blnoverallreturnvalue=false

                Exit for
        End If


    Next
```

```
        Else

            blnoverallreturnvalue=false

            Call createTestCaseLog("count
of control values and control names are
not macthing",2)
    End If



setGenericFieldvalues=blnoverallreturnv
alue

End Function
```

As seen in previous function, we can use same function to enter the data in any object in the application.
In the similar way, we can create a function that will verify the data in the application.

3.3 Main driver script

This is the entry point of the framework. This driver script will initialize all global variables. It will read environment variables if any.
This script will drive the execution of functional test cases. We are going to store the test cases in the Excel sheet. Driver script will read all test cases one by one and then execute them.
Driver script will perform below activities.

1. Read the Keyword and related test parameters of test cases from Test Data sheet.
2. Each keyword in the test case is mapped to the function in the function library in our framework.
3. Driver script will call the functionality specific function in the keyword library corresponding to the keyword in the test case.
4. All the actions that QTP is performing are logged into the html file using reporting module as and when particular keyword is executing.
5. When the function (Keyword) is executed, it returns the true or false boolean value based upon the execution status of the function. If the function is executed successfully, it returns true otherwise It returns false flag.
6. Driver script also keeps the pass and fail counters to record how many test cases have passed and how many have failed.

Here is the complete source code of the driver script in framework.

```
'*****************************************
'Global Variables Declaration
'*****************************************
dim
gintTotalRows,gTempDataTable,gfilestamp
,gTestCaseLog,gblnTestCaseStatus

Dim gActiveObject
Dim
gObjectTypes,gObjectNames,gObjectValues
```

```
'********************************************
'Function Name :- launchTest
'Function Description :- Reads the ini
file and loops through all sheets to be
executed.
'Develeoped by :- qtp-interview-
questions.blogspot.com
'********************************************

Function launchTest()


'Get the Test Parent directory
Environment.Value("TestDirectory") =
replace(Environment("TestDir"),"TestCon
troller","")
          Environment.LoadFromFile
Environment.Value("TestDirectory") &
"Environment Variable/Env.ini"

'Get the sheet where test data is
stored
          strSheetNames =
Environment.Value("SheetNames")

'Initialize the result directory path

     Environment("ResultFolderPath") =
Environment.Value("TestDirectory") &
"Results\" & formatdatetime(now,2)

     Environment("ResultFolderPath") =
```

```
replace(Environment("ResultFolderPath")
,"/","-")

'Create the report folder if it does
not exist
            CreateReportFolder()

            gfilestamp =
replace(replace(formatdatetime(now),":"
,"-"),"/","-")


'initialize the pass/fail counter.

            intTestCaseCount = 0
            intFailCount = 0

'If there are multiple datasheets,
split them and then execute each sheet
one by one

            If instr(strSheetNames,"|")
> 0  Then
                    arrSheets =
Split(strSheetNames,"|")
            Else
                    arrSheets =
Array(strSheetNames)
            End If

            For i=0 to
ubound(arrSheets)
```

```
    SheetStartTime=Now()

    activeSheet=arrSheets(i)

    intTestCaseCount=0

    gTempDataTable="New"

    tmpSheetLocation=Environment.Value("TestDirectory") & "Test Data\" & Environment.Value("Datasheet") & ".xls"


    DataTable.AddSheet gTempDataTable

'Import the data sheet in the datatable

    DataTable.ImportSheet tmpSheetLocation,arrSheets(i),gTempDataTable

'get the Total number of rows in the datasheet

    gintTotalRows=DataTable.GetSheet(gTempDataTable).GetRowCount

                    dtRows=1

                    Call
createTestCaseLog("---Executing the
```

```
Excel Sheet " & activeSheet & " ----
",4)


'Execute the test cases in the given
datasheet.
                        Call
executeSheet(SheetStartTime,activeSheet
)


'Repeat for each sheet.
            Next


End Function

'*********************************
'Function Name :- executeSheet
'Function Description :- Executes all
test cases from the given sheet
'Develeoped by :- qtp-interview-
questions.blogspot.com
'*********************************

Function
executeSheet(SheetStartTime,activeSheet
)


    intFailCount=0
    intTestCaseCount=0
```

```
    For dtrows=1 to gintTotalRows

        ' Read Test case data

strExecutionflag=trim(ucase(DataTable("
Exec_Flag",gTempDataTable)))

strExecutionflag=Replace(strExecutionfl
ag,chr(13), "")

strExecutionflag=Replace(strExecutionfl
ag, chr(10), "")

'if the execution flag is Y, execute
the test case, else jump to next test
case
        If ucase
(trim(strExecutionflag))="Y" Then

                    blnteststepflag=true

gblnTestCaseStatus=true

'read the id of current test case

strtestcaseID=datatable("ID",gTempDataT
able)

'Read the name of current test case

strtest_case_name=dataTable("test_case_
name",gTempDataTable)
```

```
                    gTestCaseLog=""
'Reinitialize the log for new test case

'loop to Execute all steps in the test
cases

 Do while     blnteststepflag

'read test step Id

strtest_step_ID=DataTable("Test_step_ID
",gTempDataTable)

'Read step description

strtest_case_steps=datatable("Test_case
_steps",gTempDataTable)

'Read Object Types


gObjectTypes=dataTable("objectTypes",gT
empDataTable)

'Read Object Names

gObjectNames=datatable("objectnames",gT
empDataTable)

'Read Object Values

gObjectValues=datatable("objectvalues",
gTempDataTable)
```

```
strscenarioname=datatable("Test_case_st
eps",gTempDataTable)

'Read Keyword name

businesskeyword=datatable("keyword",gTe
mpDataTable)

'Read Parameter1 Value

strparameter1=datatable("parameter1",gT
empDataTable)


                            Call
createTestCaseLog("-<b>" &
businesskeyword & "</b>-",4)

'Call the function mapped to keyword

ret=eval(businesskeyword)


                            If
(ret=false) or (ret="") Then

gblnTestCaseStatus=false
                            Call
createTestCaseLog("Function " &
businesskeyword & " was not
successful<br/>",2)
```

```
                              Else
                                  Call
createTestCaseLog("Function " &
businesskeyword & " was successful",1)
                              End If


'Goto next row

datatable.GetSheet(gTempDataTable).setN
extRow

     dtRows=dtRows+1

'If the test case either fails or
passes, generate the report

If datatable("ID",gTempDataTable)<>""or
datatable("keyword",gTempDataTable)=""
Then

blnteststepflag=false

datatable.GetSheet(gTempDataTable).setp
revRow

dtrows=dtrows-1
                              Call
GenerateDetailedHtmlReport(intTestCaseC
ount,strtestcaseID,strtest_case_name,gb
lnTestCaseStatus,gTestCaseLog,activeShe
et)
```

```
                        End If

'Repeat for each step in test case
'This loop ends when test case
execution is completed.

                  Loop

'update pass/fail counters

intTestCaseCount= intestcasecount+1
                      If
gblnTestCaseStatus=false Then

intFailCount=intFailCount+1
                          End If
                End If


datatable.GetSheet(gTempDataTable).setN
extRow

'Repeat for all rows in datasheet

    Next

    TestEndTime=Now()

'Find the total execution time of all
the test cases in the datasheet

        durationoftestExecution=datediff(
"n",SheetStartTime,testendtime)
```

```
'Open the report when test execution is
over

      systemutil.Run
environment.Value("ResultFolderPath")
&"\"& "Detailed" & activeSheet
&gfilestamp & ".html"


End Function
```

3.4 Object Repository

Object repository is an important part of the framework. We usually create a shared object repository.
When the application is very big, it is always good practise to create a shared repository so that multiple people can work on same verion of repository.

Creating a Shared Object Repository in QTP.
Please follow the steps given below to create a shared Object Repository in QTP.

1. Open Local Or
2. Go to File->Export Local Objects
3. Save file as abc.tsr

So abc.tsr will be a shared OR and we can associate it with any test.

Associating Shared Object Repository to QTP Test

Well - we can associate object repository to QTP Test either manually or by automation code.

Manually with Test Settings - In this method you have to go to Resources->Associate repositories. Here you can give the path of tsr file that is Shared OR.

By Automation Code, You have to use repositories collection object as mentioned in below code.

```
Dim QTPAPP
Dim qtObjRes

Set QTPAPP=
CreateObject("QuickTest.Application")
QTPAPP.Launch
QTPAPP.Visible = True

QTPAPP.Open "C:\Test\Testabc", False,
False

Set qtObjRes = QTPAPP.Test.Actions
("Login").ObjectRepositories

qtObjRes.Add "C:\OR\myRes.tsr", 1
```

More information on RepositoriesCollection Object

RepositoriesCollection Object is used to associate or disassociate shared object repositories to QTP at run time

At the beginning of a run session, the RepositoriesCollection object contains the same set of object repository files as the Associated Repository Files tab of the Action Properties dialog box. The operations you perform on the RepositoriesCollection object affect only the run-time copy of the collection.

You use the RepositoriesCollection object to associate or disassociate shared object repositories with an action during a run session.

RepositoriesCollection Methods

Add   - Add .tsr file to current action in test

Find - Find the index position of .tsr file in collection

MoveToPos - Change the position of repository

Remove   - Remove repository from current action in test

RemoveAll - Remove all repositories from current action in test

RepositoriesCollection Properties

Count   - Get the total number of .tsr files associated to current action in test

Item   - gets the path of the tsr file located in the specified index position.

 We can add any number of .tsr files to current action in test at run time.

Example -

```
RepPath = "c:\Mercury\my.tsr"

RepositoriesCollection.RemoveAll()

RepositoriesCollection.Add(RepPath)

Pos =
RepositoriesCollection.Find(RepPath)

RepositoriesCollection.Remove(Pos)

RepositoriesCollection.Add(RepPath)
' add tsr filr

Window("Microso").WinObject("my").Click

Pos =
RepositoriesCollection.Find(RepPath)
```

3.5 Reporting

Now let us look at the reporting part of the framework. We are creating html reports for the automation execution. You must know basics of HTML and CSS to understand how reports are created in QTP.

To create html reports, we simply write html data along with test execution log to text file and then change the extention of the file to .html

Please have a look at below reports.

No	Test_Case_id	Test_Case_Name	Test_Case_Log
0	1	insert order	Info :--login-- Pass:Login was successful Pass:Login was successful Pass:functionlogin was successful Info :--insertorder-- Pass:insert order was successful Pass:functioninsertorder was successful

```
'* * * * * * * * * * * * * * * * * * * * * * * * * * * * * * * * *
'Function Name :-
generateDetailedHTMLReport
'Function Description :- generate
detailed report
'Develeoped by :- qtp-interview-
questions.blogspot.com
'* * * * * * * * * * * * * * * * * * * * * * * * * * * * * * * * *


Function
generateDetailedHTMLReport(byval
intTestCaseCount,byval
strTestCaseID,byval
strTest_Case_Name,byval
OverallTestCaseStatus,byval
testlog,byval l_strsheetname)
```

```
If OverallTestCaseStatus=False Then
        OverallTestCaseStatus="<span
style=""color:red"">Fail</span>"

    Else

        OverallTestCaseStatus="<span
style=""color:green"">Pass</span>"
    End If

    If intTestCaseCount=0 Then

strDetailedHTML="<html><head><title>Det
ailed Report Of Execution </title><link
rel=""stylesheet"" type=""text/css""
href=""" & "..\styles.css""></head>
<body><table><tr><th>No</th><th>Test_Ca
se_id</th><th>Test_Case_Name</th><th>Te
st_Case_Log</th><th>Test_Case_Status</t
h></tr>"
        filepath="Detailed" &
l_strsheetname & gfilestamp & ".html"
        Call
AppendToFile(filepath,strDetailedHTML)
    End If
        strDetailedHTML="<tr><td>" &
intTestCaseCount & "</td><td>" &
strTestCaseID & "</td><td> "&
strTest_Case_Name & "</td><td
style=""text-align:left;""> " & testlog
& "</td><td>" & OverallTestCaseStatus &
"</td></tr>"
```

```
                filepath="Detailed" &
l_strSheetname & gfilestamp & ".html"
        Call
AppendToFile(filepath,strDetailedHtml)
End Function




'* * * * * * * * * * * * * * * * * * * * * * * * * * * * * * * * * * * * *
'Function Name :- AppendToFile
'Function Description :- Append to file
'Develeoped by :- qtp-interview-
questions.blogspot.com
'* * * * * * * * * * * * * * * * * * * * * * * * * * * * * * * * * * * * *


Function AppendToFile(byval
filepath,byval contents)


filepath=Environment.Value("ResultFolde
rPath") & "\" & filepath
    Set
Fo=createobject("Scripting.FileSystemOb
ject")
    Set
f=Fo.OpenTextFile(filepath,8,true)
    f.Write(contents)
    f.Close
    Set f=nothing
End Function




'* * * * * * * * * * * * * * * * * * * * * * * * * * * * * * * * * * * * *
'Function Name :- CreateTestCaseLog
```

```
'Function Description :-
CreateTestCaseLog
'Develeoped by :- qtp-interview-
questions.blogspot.com
'*******************************

Function
CreateTestCaseLog(str,intStatus)

   If intStatus=1 Then
        strhtml="<span
style=""color:green"">Pass:</span>"

        Elseif  intStatus=2 Then
        strhtml="<span
style=""color:red""> Fail :</span>"

        Elseif intStatus=3 Then
        strhtml="<span
style=""color:gray""> Warning :
</span>"

        Elseif intStatus=4 Then
        strhtml="<span>Info
 :</span>"
   End If

   gtestcaselog=gtestcaselog & strhtml
& str & "<br/>"
End Function


'*******************************
```

```
'Function Name :- CreateReportFolder
'Function Description :-
CreateReportFolder
'Develeoped by :- qtp-interview-
questions.blogspot.com
'*****************************************

Function CreateReportFolder()

    Set
Fo=createobject("Scripting.FilesystemOb
ject")
    If Not
Fo.FolderExists(Environment.Value("Resu
ltFolderPath")) Then

Fo.CreateFolder(Environment.Value("Resu
ltFolderPath"))
    End If
End Function

'*****************************************
'Function Name :- GenerateFinalReports
'Function Description :-
GenerateFinalReports
'Develeoped by :- qtp-interview-
questions.blogspot.com
'*****************************************

Function GenerateFinalReports(byval
intTestCaseCount,byval
intFailCount,byval
```

```
DurationOfTestExecution,byval
sheetName)

    intPassCount=intTestCaseCount-
intFailCount


strGraphs="<br/><hr/><table><tr><th>TcE
xecuted</th><th>TC Passed</th><th>TC
Failed</th><th>TC Execution
Time</th></tr>"

    strGraphs=strGraphs & "<tr><th>" &
intTestCaseCount & "</th><th>" &
intPassCount &"</th><th>" &
intFailCount & "</th><th>" &
DurationOfTestEecution &
"<th></tr></table>"

'for Detailed

strDetailedHTML="</table></body></html>
"
filepath="Detailed" & sheetName &
gfilestamp & ".html"

Call
AppendToFile(filepath,strDetailedHTML)


End Function
```

4. Hybrid Automation framework

In this chapter, you will learn about how to design hybrdi automation frameworks in QTP.

4.1 Hybrid framework Introduction

Hybrid framework is the combination of data driven and keyword driven frameworks. We have already seen how we can develop data driven and keyword driven framework. Hybrid framework used the few or all features of both the frameworks to create better framework.

4.2 Hybrid framework features

The Hybrid-Driven Testing pattern is made up of a number of reusable modules / function libraries that are developed with the following characteristics in mind:

- Maintainability – significantly reduces the test maintenance effort
- Reusability – due to modularity of test cases and library functions
- Reliability – due to advanced error handling and scenario recovery
- Measurability – customisable reporting of test results ensure quality

5. Utility Functions in frameworks

In this chapter, you will get to know some of the important utility functions that can be used in QTP framework.

Before you start developing the automation frameworks, you must know some basic utility functions in QTP. Let us have a look at some of the most important utilities in QTP.

5.1 Reading Excel File in QTP.

As our test datasheet is stored in Excel file, we must know how to read and write the excel file.

Below code will illustrate how we can read Excel file in QTP.

```
'Set the excel file path
filepath = "C:\Bugs\Report.xlsx"

'Create excel application object
Set objExcel =
CreateObject("Excel.Application")

'Make excel application visible
objExcel.Visible = True

'Open the workbook
Set Wb =
objExcel.Workbooks.Open(filepath)
```

```
'Print the value in Cell A1
print Wb.worksheets(1).Cells(1,1).Value
```

5.2 Changing the date format

In all banking projects, we need to work with dates. We need to convert the format of dates. So we can write a generic function which will change the date format as required. Also we need to find the future and past dates.

Here is the sample GetDate function which will find future and past date as well as It will change the date format.

Below function will return the date in mm/dd/yyyy format.
Call Getdate("T") - will return todays date
Call Getdate("T+1") - will return tommorow's date
Call Getdate("T-1") - Will return previous day's date.
You can calculate any future or past date with this example.

```
Function GetDate(byval curvalue)
    If ucase(curvalue) = "T" Then
        curvalue = curvalue & "+0"
    End If

If instr(1,curvalue,"+") > 0 Then
  arrdate = split(curvalue,"+")
'Get future date

    retDate = dateadd("d",arrdate(1),now)
```

```
  'Get month part of date

strmonth = month(cdate(retDate))

'Get day part of the date

strday = day(cdate(retDate))

'Get year part of the date

stryear = year(cdate(retDate))

        If len(strmonth) = 1 Then
        strmonth = "0" & strmonth
        End If

        If len(strday) = 1 Then
          strday = "0" & strday
        End If
Else

        arrdate = split(curvalue,"-")
        curDate = - cint(arrdate(1))
'Get past date
      retDate = dateadd("d",curDate,now)

    strmonth = month(cdate(retDate))
    strday = day(cdate(retDate))
    stryear = year(cdate(retDate))

    If len(strmonth) = 1 Then
```

```
        strmonth = "0" & strmonth
    End If

    If len(strday) = 1 Then
        strday = "0" & strday
    End If


End If

'change the date format

    If Ucase(strParameter1) = "YYYY-MM-
DD" Then
        GetDate = stryear & "-" &
strmonth & "-" & strday
    Else
        GetDate = strmonth & "/" &
strday & "/" & stryear
    End If


End Function
```

5.3 Writing Data to Text File

To create html reports, we have to write the test log to text file.
We can use filesystem object to work with files in QTP.
Below Code will write data to text file in QTP.

```
'Content to be written to file
        content = "This will be in file "

'Create file System Object
        Set Fo =
createobject("Scripting.FilesystemObjec
t")

'open the file in Append mode
        Set f =
Fo.openTextFile("c:\abc.txt",8,true)

'Write the contents to the end of the
file.
        f.Write (contents)

'Close the file
        f.Close

'release the resources.
        Set f = nothing
```

This is how we can write the data to the text file in QTP.

5.4 Associating Library file to QTP Test

In frameworks we create a separate library files (vbs/qfl). So we must associate these files to QTP test.

Well - we can associate function library to QTP Test either manually or by automation code.

Manually with Test Settings - In this method you have to go to **Test Settings->Resources** and add any library file. Library File can have 3 extentions - .vbs, .qfl or .txt

By Automation Code, You have to use below code.

```
'Create QTP Application object

    Set App =
CreateObject("QuickTest.Application")

    If App.Launched Then
'If QuickTest is  open
            App.Quit
    End If

'Launch application
    App.Launch

'Make QTP visible
    App.Visible = True

'open QTP Test
    App.Open Testpath

'Get the libraries collection
    Set qtplib =
App.Test.Settings.Resources.Libraries
```

```
     qtplib.RemoveAll

'Add the library file located
     qtplib.add "c:\lib1.vbs"

'Save the test
     App.Test.Save
```

5.5 Associating Object Repository file to QTP Test

Well - we can associate object repository to QTP Test either manually or by automation code.

Manually with Test Settings - In this method you have to go to Resources->Associate repositories. Here you can give the path of tsr file that is Shared OR.

By Automation Code, You have to use repositories collection object as mentioned in below code.

```
Dim QTPAPP
Dim qtObjRes

Set QTPAPP=
CreateObject("QuickTest.Application")
QTPAPP.Launch
QTPAPP.Visible = True

QTPAPP.Open "C:\Test\Testabc", False,
False
```

```
'Get repositories collection object
Set qtObjRes = QTPAPP.Test.Actions
("Login").ObjectRepositories

'Add tsr file
qtObjRes.Add "C:\OR\myRes.tsr", 1
```

5.6 Closing processes by Name

It is very frequent requirement that we need to close particular application before running the test.
Below code will show you how to close all internet explorer browsers in QTP.

```
Function closeIE()


sComp = "."


'Get the WMI object
                                    Set
WMI = GetObject("winmgmts:\\" &    sComp
&  "\root\cimv2")


'Get collection of processes for with
name iexplore.exe
                                    Set
allIE = WMI.ExecQuery("Select * from
```

```
Win32_Process Where Name =
'iexplore.exe'")


'Loop through each process and
terminate it
                                    For
Each IE in allIE

IE.Terminate()

Next

End Function
```

Similarly we can close any process by its name. You will have to change the name of the process in above code.

5.7 Sending an email from framework

The stakeholders involved in the automation projects have to be informed on the automation execution status. We can do it by sending an email whenever execution ends.

Here is the sample code to send mail from outlook client in QTP.

```
'Create outlook object
Set Outlook =
CreateObject("Outlook.Application")

Dim Message 'As Outlook.MailItem
```

```
'create a new mail/message object
Set Message = Outlook.CreateItem(0)

With Message
'Set the subject
        .Subject = Subject
'Set the body of mail
        .HTMLBody = TextBody
'Add the recipients
        .Recipients.Add
("abcxyz44@gmail.com")

'Send mail
        .Send
End With
```

5.8 Taking a screenshot in QTP.

In QTP, when we execute the test cases, test cases may fail due to valid / invalid defects. They may also fail due to script issues or any other issues like network failure.

After the test execution ends, We only have the html reports or QTP results with us which does not give clear picture about the status of application. To solve this problem we can take the snapshot of the application when any test step fails.

Example - Below code will take the screen shot. You can insert this code anywhere you want to take the screen shot.

```
Window("xyz").CaptureBitmap
"c:\screenshots\abc.png", True
```

In above code we are storing the png image file to c drive location. Second parameter tells whether to overwrite existing file.

Thus you can use capturebitmap method of any object to take the screen shot.

5.9 Importing excel sheet to datatable in qtp

When we design a test automation framework in qtp, we usually store the test data inside excel sheets.
Sometimes we need to load the test data in datatable to execute the test cases.

We can either import all excel sheets from excel workbook or we can import particular excel sheet from the the workbook to the datatable

To import all sheets from excel file, use below line of code

```
datatable.Import "c:\abc.xls"
```

To import single sheet from excel file, use below line of code here we are importing the sheet global from abc.xls into testdata sheet in datatable in QTP.

```
datatable.AddSheet "testdata"
```

```
datatable.ImportSheet
"c:\abc.xls","Global","testdata"
```

5.10 Exporting the datatable sheets

Working with datatable is very common in QTP.
We use datatables to store the runtime data.

The biggest disadvantage of datatable is that it is a temporary storage which means that data stored in datatable is removed when test execution is over.

If you want to reserve the datatable data, you can export the data to excel sheet so that you can use it later on.

Examples -

```
'Add some data to global sheet in
datatable
datatable.GlobalSheet.AddParameter
"p1","v"
datatable("p1") = "abc"

'Export complete datatable - This will
export all sheets from the datatable
datatable.Export("c:\abc.xls")

'export only particular sheet from the
datatable to excel sheet
```

```
'after below code is executed, sheet
with name global will be exported to
excel sheet in kk.xls
datatable.ExportSheet
"c:\kk.xls","Global"
```

5.11 Loading ini file in QTP

Ini files are used to store global data required for testing.

Typical ini file looks like this.

[Environment]
   URL=http://xyz.com
   UserId=abc
   Password=pass

 [Environment]

Example -

To load above ini file in QTP script, you have to use below lines of code

```
Environment.LoadFromFile
"c:\Environment_Variable\Env.ini"

Print  Environment.Value("URL")
```

This is how you can read values from ini file in QTP.

www.ingramcontent.com/pod-product-compliance
Lightning Source LLC
Chambersburg PA
CBHW061036050326
40689CB00012B/2858